Britain and the
United Nations

or before

London: H M S O

Researched and written by Reference Services, Central Office of Information.

ISBN 0 11 701866 X

HMSO publications are available from:

HMSO Publications Centre
(Mail, fax and telephone orders only)
PO Box 276, London SW8 5DT
Telephone orders 0171-873 9090
General enquiries 0171-873 0011
(queuing system in operation for both numbers)
Fax orders 0171-873 8200

HMSO Bookshops
49 High Holborn, London WC1V 6HB
0171-873 0011   Fax 0171-873 8200 (counter service only)
68–69 Bull Street, Birmingham, B4 6AD   0121–236 9696   Fax 0121–236 9699
33 Wine Street, Bristol BS1 2BQ   0117 926 4306   Fax 0177 9294515
9-21 Princess Street, Manchester M60 8AS
0161-834 7201   Fax 0161-833 0634
16 Arthur Street, Belfast BT1 4GD   01232 238451   Fax 01232 235401
71 Lothian Road, Edinburgh EH3 9AZ   0131-228 4181   Fax 0131-229 2734

HMSO's Accredited Agents
(see Yellow Pages)

and through good booksellers

Contents

Acknowledgments

The Central Office of Information would like to thank the Foreign and Commonwealth Office for its co-operation in compiling this book.

Cover Photograph Credit
COI Pictures.

Introduction

Britain[1] believes in the maintenance of a stable international order governed by respect for agreed international law. Commitment to the purposes and principles of the United Nations (UN) and its Charter has therefore been the cornerstone of British policy since 1945. In Britain's view, all UN member states should ensure that the organisation functions effectively to maintain peace and international security, assist developing countries and promote respect for human rights and fundamental freedoms.

This book describes the role and structure of the UN and examines Britain's involvement in the organisation's evolution and operations.

---

[1] The term 'Britain' is used in this book to mean the United Kingdom of Great Britain and Northern Ireland; 'Great Britain' comprises England, Wales and Scotland.

Formation of the United Nations

The outbreak of the Second World War in 1939 marked the failure of the League of Nations, formed after the First World War, to sustain a stable and lasting peace. Recognising the need to establish more effective post-war arrangements, Britain and the United States issued the Atlantic Charter in August 1941, to which the then Soviet Union and other allied countries at war with Germany, Italy and Japan subscribed in a 'United Nations Declaration' of 1 January 1942. The Atlantic Charter looked forward to 'a peace which will afford to all nations the means of dwelling in safety within their own boundaries', to 'freedom from fear and want', disarmament of the aggressors and the creation of 'a wider and permanent system of general security'.

In October 1943 Britain, China, the Soviet Union and the United States signed the Moscow Declaration advocating 'a general international organisation, based on the principle of the sovereign equality of all peace-loving states and open to membership of all such states, large and small, for the maintenance of international peace and security'. Detailed plans were worked out between representatives of the allied powers in the autumn of 1944 at the Dumbarton Oaks Conference in the United States. These were largely embodied in the subsequent Charter of the UN.

The UN Charter

The Charter (see Appendix, p. 59) was signed by 51 countries at a conference in San Francisco in June 1945. It came into force in October of that year following ratification by a majority of the original signatories, including Britain, China, France, the Soviet Union and the United States.

Basic Purposes and Principles

The UN is based on the principle of the sovereign equality of all its members. The purposes of the organisation are defined by the Charter as:

—the maintenance of international peace and security;

—the settlement of international disputes in conformity with justice and international law;

—the development of friendly relations among nations based upon respect for equal rights and the self-determination of peoples;

—the achievement of international co-operation in solving international economic, social, cultural and humanitarian problems; and

—the promotion and encouragement of respect for human rights and fundamental freedoms without discrimination as to race, sex, language or religion.

UN members are committed under the Charter to refrain from the threat or use of force against the territorial integrity or political independence of any state and to settle their disputes by peaceful means. In addition, all members are required to assist the UN in any action it takes in accordance with the Charter and to refrain from assisting any state against which the organisation is taking preventive or enforcement action.

The Charter recognises and permits the right of individual or collective self-defence against armed attack and the existence of regional arrangements designed to maintain peace and security.

The UN is not authorised to intervene in the internal affairs of a sovereign state, but this principle does not prejudice the application of enforcement measures agreed by the UN Security Council (see p. 6).

Membership of the organisation is open to all peace-loving states which accept the obligations of the Charter. New members are admitted by the UN General Assembly on the recommendation of the Security Council. The original membership of 51 has grown to 184. The Charter provides for the suspension or expulsion of a member state on the recommendation of the Security Council for violation of the principles of the Charter, but no such action has ever been taken since the establishment of the organisation.

Organs of the United Nations

The six principal organs of the UN, established by the Charter, are described below.

The Security Council

The Security Council has primary responsibility for maintaining international peace and security, and to that end it acts for all UN members (Article 24 of the Charter). It can be convened at any time whenever peace is threatened and member states are sometimes obligated to carry out its decisions in accordance with the Charter.

The Council has five permanent members—Britain, France, the People's Republic of China, Russia and the United States. The other ten member countries are elected by the General Assembly for two-year terms. Five of the elective seats are allocated to Africa and Asia, one to eastern Europe, two to Latin America and two to western Europe and certain other countries. Each Council member state holds the Presidency for one month, the rotation following the English alphabetical order. A working group, in which Britain is playing an active part, is looking at the question of enlarging the Council.

Decisions by the Security Council require nine affirmative votes. Except in votes on procedural matters, a decision cannot be taken if there is a 'no' vote by a permanent Council member (known as the 'veto'). If a permanent member does not support a decision but does not wish to block it through a veto, it may abstain.

Functions and Powers

When a complaint concerning a possible threat to peace is brought before the Council, it usually first asks the parties to reach agreement by peaceful means. In some cases it may propose mediation or set out principles for a settlement. When a dispute leads to fighting, the Council tries to secure a ceasefire. It may send peacekeeping units—observers or troops—to troubled areas to reduce tensions and help maintain the ceasefire.

To enforce its decisions, the Security Council has the power to impose economic and other sanctions and authorise collective military action under Chapter VII of the Charter (see p. 68). The Charter envisaged members placing at the disposal of the Council armed forces and other facilities which would be co-ordinated by the Military Staff Committee, composed of military representatives of the five permanent members. Because of the cold war, the Security Council was for many years unable to function fully in the ways intended by the Charter. The Military Staff Committee was effectively suspended from 1948 to 1990, when a meeting was convened during the Gulf crisis (see p. 31) on the formation and control of UN-supervised armed forces.

The Security Council makes recommendations to the General Assembly on a candidate for UN Secretary General and on the admission of new members to the organisation.

The General Assembly

The General Assembly is the main deliberative body. It is composed of all member states, each of which has one vote. Decisions on ordinary matters are reached by a simple majority. More important questions, such as recommendations relating to peace and security, require a two-thirds majority.

The Assembly meets in regular session throughout most of the year. Special or emergency sessions can be held if necessary. Its work is also carried on in a number of special committees and bodies.

The Assembly can discuss and make recommendations on all matters within the scope of the UN Charter. Although it does not have the power to compel action by any government, its recommendations can carry the weight of world opinion as well as the moral authority of the world community.

In addition to setting policies and determining programmes for the UN Secretariat (see below), the Assembly may call for world conferences on major issues and designate 'international years' to focus attention on specific topics. It also considers reports from other organs, admits new members, approves the budget and appoints the UN Secretary General.

If the Security Council is unable to take action because of a veto by one of the permanent members, in a case which appears to be a threat to the peace, breach of the peace or act of aggression, the General Assembly may take action under the 1950 Uniting for Peace procedure. Under this procedure, which was used in 1950 as a result of North Korea's invasion of South Korea, the Assembly is empowered to consider the question immediately with a view to making recommendations to member states for collective action; in the case of armed aggression this can include the use of armed force to maintain or restore international peace and security. Two-thirds of Assembly members must approve the recommendation.

The UN Secretariat

The Secretariat services the other organs of the UN and administers the programmes and policies laid down by them. At its head is the Secretary General, who is appointed by the General Assembly on the recommendation of the Security Council.

Made up of an international staff drawn from some 160 countries, the Secretariat carries out the day-to-day work of the UN. As international civil servants they work for the UN as a whole, and pledge not to seek or receive instructions from any government or outside authority.

The Secretary-General may bring to the attention of the Security Council any matter which, in his opinion, threatens peace and security. He plays an important role in peacemaking, both personally and through special representatives or teams which he may appoint for specific purposes, such as negotiation or fact-finding.

The work of the Secretariat includes:

—administering peacekeeping operations;

—organising international conferences on problems of worldwide concern;

—surveying world economic and social trends; and

—preparing studies on such subjects as human rights, disarmament and development.

The Economic and Social Council

In the economic and social fields, the UN is charged by its Charter with promoting:

—higher standards of living, full employment, and conditions of economic and social progress and development;

—the solution of international economic, social, health and related problems;

—international cultural and educational co-operation; and

—universal respect for, and observance of, human rights and fundamental freedoms.

The Economic and Social Council (ECOSOC) is responsible for discharging these functions under the authority of the General Assembly. ECOSOC is made up of 54 UN member states, which are elected for a three-year term. Eighteen members are elected each year.

The functions of ECOSOC are to:

—make or initiate studies and reports on international economic, social, cultural, educational, health and related matters;

—make recommendations on such matters to the General Assembly, to members of the UN, and to the specialised agencies concerned;

—make recommendations for promoting respect for, and observance of, human rights;

—prepare draft conventions for submission to the General Assembly and call international conferences on matters within its competence; and

— enter into agreements with specialised agencies and consult with non-governmental organisations.

Trusteeship Council

The Charter set up an International Trusteeship System and assigned to the Trusteeship Council the task of supervising the administration of territories placed under that system. Such territories had been dependencies of powers defeated in the Second World War and were placed under UN trusteeship with the object of leading them, through political, economic, social and educational development, to self-government and independence.

The Council is the only UN organ whose activities have diminished over the years. Because of the extent of its accomplishments, only one of the 11 original trusteeships, Palau—part of the Trust Territory of the Pacific Islands—now remains. All other trust territories have attained self-government and independence, either as separate states or by joining neighbouring independent countries.

As the number of administering countries has diminished so has the size of the Council. There are now only five members: the United States (as the administering state in the case of Palau) and the other permanent members of the UN Security Council. The Council meets in annual session, each member having one vote.

International Court of Justice

The main judicial organ of the UN is the International Court of Justice (also known as the World Court) which sits at The Hague in The Netherlands. It functions in accordance with a Statute annexed to the UN Charter and is permanently in session.

Only states may be parties in cases brought before the Court. The Court is open to all members of the UN. The jurisdiction of the Court covers all legal disputes which are referred to it by states. However, the Court can hear a case only if both parties to the dispute agree to this step being taken. The Court may also give advisory opinions to the UN.

The Court consists of 15 judges (including one from Britain) elected by the UN General Assembly and the Security Council, voting independently. They are chosen on the basis of their qualifications, not on the basis of nationality. No two judges may be nationals of the same state. Judges serve for a term of nine years and may be re-elected.

Although the Court normally sits in plenary session, it may also form smaller units called chambers if the parties so request. Judgments given by chambers are considered as rendered by the full Court.

Specialised and Other Intergovernmental Agencies

The specialised and other intergovernmental agencies related to the UN by special agreements are separate, autonomous organisations which work with the UN and each other. They have wide international responsibilities for the promotion of economic, social, educational, health and cultural progress.

Specialised Agencies

Each specialised agency has a different relationship with the General Assembly and ECOSOC. They are mainly independent in operational terms but have links with various parts of the UN system. Britain is a member of all but the UN Educational, Scientific and Cultural Organisation (UNESCO).

International Labour Organisation (ILO)

The ILO, which has existed since 1919, became the first UN specialised agency in 1946. It adopts conventions and recommendations which set international labour standards in such areas as freedom of association, wages, hours and conditions of work, social insurance and industrial safety.

The ILO also provides technical assistance to member countries with regard to vocational training, management techniques, manpower planning, employment policies and occupational health and safety.

Food and Agriculture Organisation (FAO)

The FAO was set up in 1945. Its aims are to raise levels of nutrition and standards of living and to improve the production, processing, marketing and distribution of food and agricultural products. It also encourages rural development.

In carrying out these aims, the FAO promotes investment in agricultural practice and the transfer of technology to, and development of agricultural research in, developing countries. It also promotes the conservation of natural resources, the development of fisheries and of renewable energy sources and the rational use of forests. Special FAO programmes help countries prepare for, and provide relief in the event of, emergency food situations.

United Nations Educational, Scientific and Cultural Organisation (UNESCO)

Britain supports the objectives contained in UNESCO's constitution, which are to promote collaboration between nations through education, science, culture and communication. However, Britain withdrew from the organisation in 1985 because of doubts about the effectiveness with which UNESCO had pursued its aims.

After a detailed review of UNESCO activities, Britain announced in 1990 that the reforms carried out were not yet sufficient to merit rejoining. The funds saved from the withdrawal are allocated to a number of bilateral aid programmes.

World Health Organisation (WHO)

The WHO was established in 1948. It aims to raise the standard of health of all peoples to the highest possible level. The strategy to achieve this objective is based on the promotion of primary health care, focusing on health education, proper food supply and nutrition, safe water and sanitation, maternal and child health including family planning, control and prevention of disease and the provision of essential drugs and medical supplies. The WHO administers research programmes and provides member countries with advisory services and technical assistance.

Britain is supporting the work of the WHO in co-ordinating international efforts to prevent and control Acquired Immune Deficiency Syndrome (AIDS). It has contributed over £33 million to the WHO Global Programme on AIDS, and is also providing funds through the WHO for medium-term AIDS control plans in Africa, Asia and the Caribbean.

International Civil Aviation Organisation (ICAO)

The ICAO, which was set up in 1947, aims to ensure the safe and orderly growth of civil aviation and to encourage the design and operation of aircraft for peaceful purposes. Other objectives are to support the development of airways, airports and air-navigation facilities for civil aviation and to meet the needs of the international public for safe and efficient air transport.

Universal Postal Union (UPU)

The UPU was established in 1874 by a treaty approved by 22 nations at Berne in Switzerland. It became a specialised agency of the UN in 1948.

The organisation forms a single postal territory of countries for the reciprocal exchange of letter-post items. Its functions are to secure the improvement of the postal services and to promote international collaboration in postal matters as well as technical co-operation.

International Telecommunication Union (ITU)

Originating in 1865, the ITU became a UN specialised agency in 1947. Its main purposes are to extend international co-operation for the improvement of telecommunications of all kinds and to promote the development of technical facilities and their most efficient operation.

World Meteorological Organisation (WMO)

The objectives of the WMO, as defined in a convention which came into effect in 1950, are to facilitate worldwide co-operation in establishing networks of stations for meteorological observations and to promote the rapid exchange of weather information. The organisation also aims to further the application of meteorology to aviation, shipping, agriculture and other activities, and to encourage research and training.

WMO programmes include World Weather Watch, the World Climate Programme and the Global Atmosphere Watch.

International Maritime Organisation (IMO)

The IMO was formally established as a UN specialised agency in 1959, and is the only specialised agency to be based in Britain. It provides the means for co-operation and exchange of information among governments on technical matters affecting shipping engaged in international trade. It also encourages the adoption of the highest practicable standards relating to maritime safety, navigational efficiency and marine pollution control.

World Intellectual Property Organisation (WIPO)

The organisation was set up in 1970 under a convention signed in 1967 and became a specialised agency in 1974. Its objectives are to maintain and increase respect for intellectual property throughout the world. Intellectual property comprises industrial property (inventions, trademarks and designs) and copyright.

International Fund for Agricultural Development (IFAD)

Created in 1977, the IFAD's main purpose is to mobilise resources for concessional or low-interest loans to developing countries for agricultural development projects, in order to increase food production and provide employment and additional income for poor rural communities.

United Nations Industrial Development Organisation (UNIDO)

UNIDO was set up in 1966 by the UN General Assembly in order to promote and accelerate the industrialisation of the developing countries. It became a specialised agency in 1986.

In addition to assisting developing countries in the establishment and operation of industries, UNIDO provides a forum for contacts, consultations and negotiations between developing and industrialised countries. It also encourages investment-promotion activities and facilitates the transfer of technology to and between developing countries.

Other Intergovernmental Agencies

International Atomic Energy Agency (IAEA)

Britain is a member of the IAEA, which is not a specialised agency but an independent intergovernmental organisation, established in 1957, under the aegis of the UN. The Agency is responsible for international activities regarding the peaceful uses of nuclear energy. It encourages research, fosters the exchange of scientific and technical information and provides a focus for work on international standards for nuclear safety and radiation protection. It also administers nuclear safeguards designed to ensure that fissionable and other materials are not diverted illegally to further any military purpose.

The IAEA submits reports to the UN General Assembly and, where appropriate, to the Security Council and ECOSOC.

General Agreement on Tariffs and Trade (GATT)

GATT, to which Britain is a contracting party, has been in force since 1948 and is the only multilateral instrument which lays down agreed rules for international trade. It is regarded as a *de facto* specialised agency but does not have formal status as such.

The basic aim of GATT is to liberalise world trade. It is in effect a code of rules for the conduct of trade and a forum in which countries can resolve their trade problems and negotiate to enlarge trading opportunities.

The various rounds of GATT have succeeded in lowering average tariff levels in the industrialised countries from about 40 per cent in the late 1940s to 5 per cent today. In terms of volume, world merchandise trade has multiplied 12-fold since GATT was established. In 1993 the Uruguay Round of trade negotiations was successfully concluded. In 1995 GATT will be replaced by the World Trade Organisation.

International Bank for Reconstruction and Development (IBRD/World Bank)

Agreements drawn up at the Bretton Woods financial and monetary conference in 1944, attended by 44 governments, led to the establishment in 1945 of the IBRD (and the International Monetary Fund—see p. 19). The IBRD was set up to assist in the economic reconstruction and development of member countries by making loans to governments and private enterprises for productive purposes. Its objectives are to facilitate the investment of capital and to promote private foreign investment. It also promotes the balanced growth of international trade and the maintenance of equilibrium in the balance of payments of its members.

The IBRD, whose capital is subscribed by its member countries, finances its lending operations mainly from its own borrowings in world markets, as well as from retained earnings and repayments on its loans.

International Development Association (IDA)

The IDA was set up in 1960 as an affiliate of the IBRD to provide capital for poor developing countries on easier terms. Its objectives are poverty reduction, economic reform and sustainable development. The bulk of its resources come from three sources: transfers from the IBRD's net earnings, capital subscribed in convertible currencies by IDA member states and contributions from the IDA's richer members.

Nearly all IDA 'credits', as they are called to distinguish them from IBRD 'loans', have been for a period of 50 years, without interest, except for a charge to cover administrative costs. Repayment does not begin until after a ten-year grace period.

International Finance Corporation (IFC)

The IFC was established as a separate affiliate of the IBRD in 1956. It provides and promotes investment, without government guarantee, in productive private enterprises in member countries. It also acts as a clearing house to bring together investment opportunities, private capital and experienced management. Its resources come mainly from subscriptions by its member countries and from accumulated earnings.

International Monetary Fund (IMF)

Founded in 1945 following the Bretton Woods agreement of 1944, the IMF aims to promote international monetary co-operation and the expansion of international trade through a multilateral payments system and assistance to countries facing short-term balance of payments difficulties. It seeks to promote exchange stability, maintain orderly exchange arrangements and avoid competitive exchange depreciation.

Member countries may purchase foreign exchange from the IMF to make short- or medium-term payments. Each member is assigned a quota which determines its subscription, its voting power and the amount of foreign exchange which it may purchase.

Other UN Bodies

There are a number of other agencies, programmes and funds established by the UN General Assembly which are dedicated to achieving economic and social progress in the developing countries and to which Britain is an active contributor. These include:

UN Development Programme (UNDP)

In the forefront of efforts to bring about social and economic progress is the UNDP, the world's largest multilateral grant-assistance organisation. It administers the majority of the technical assistance provided through the UN system. With an annual budget of $1,300 million, it is active in more than 150 countries and territories, co-ordinating development programmes in virtually every economic and social sector. There are over 6,000 UNDP-supported projects in operation, all aimed at helping developing countries make better use of their assets, improve living standards and expand productivity (see p. 57). Fifty-five per cent of UNDP funds for projects go to 45 of the world's poorest countries.

UN Children's Fund (UNICEF)

Established in 1946 to deliver post-war relief to children, UNICEF now concentrates its assistance on developing countries. It provides primary health care and health education, conducting programmes in oral hydration, immunisation against prevalent diseases, child-growth monitoring and the encouragement of breastfeeding. Its operations are often conducted in co-operation with the WHO.

UN High Commissioner for Refugees (UNHCR)

The Office of the UNHCR was established in 1950 to protect the rights and interests of refugees and promote durable solutions to their problems. It organises emergency relief and longer-term solutions, such as voluntary repatriation, local integration or resettlement. The work of UNHCR is of a purely humanitarian and non-political nature.

UN Relief and Works Agency for Palestine Refugees in the Near East (UNRWA)

UNRWA was created in 1949 to bring assistance to Palestinian Arab refugees and to help them become self-supporting. Its mandate has repeatedly been renewed. Education and basic health care account for about four-fifths of the agency's budget. Britain is one of the major donor countries (see p. 58).

UN Environment Programme (UNEP)

UNEP, established after the 1972 Stockholm Conference on the Environment, co-ordinates UN environmental activities, calling attention to global and regional environmental issues and stimulating programmes to address problems. It assists developing countries in implementing environmentally-sound development policies, and has produced a worldwide environmental monitoring system to standardise international data (see also p. 47).

UN Population Fund (UNFPA)

Set up in 1967, UNFPA is the largest internationally-funded source of assistance to population programmes in developing countries. The major portion of its funds, almost all of which come from voluntary governmental contributions, is allocated to family planning projects.

World Food Programme (WFP)

The WFP, established in 1961 by the UN and the FAO, distributes food commodities in support of programmes of social and economic development, for protracted refugee projects and for relief in emergency situations.

Budget and Contributions

The regular budget of the UN is approved by the General Assembly every two years. It covers expenses relating to substantive programmes, programme support and administrative activities of the organisation.

Funding for the regular budget is from contributions by member states, which are assessed on a scale specified by the General Assembly, based on capacity to pay. The Assembly has fixed a maximum of 25 per cent of the budget for any one contributor and a minimum of 0.01 per cent. Britain is the sixth largest contributor to the UN's regular budget. In 1993 its contribution was $51,229,662.

Quite separately from the regular budget, member states are also assessed for the costs of UN peacekeeping operations. Other UN activities are financed by voluntary contributions outside the regular budget.

International Peace and Security

Through the adversarial decades of the cold war, the UN Security Council was unable to function fully in the ways intended by the Charter. The end of the cold war gave the organisation a new lease of life. This process started in 1986 with the close consultations between the five permanent Council members which led ultimately to a ceasefire in the war between Iran and Iraq, but it was the role of the UN in the Gulf crisis from August 1990 (for details of which and other individual UN operations see pp. 25–32) which propelled the organisation back into the centre of world politics.

'Agenda for Peace'

In January 1992 Britain, as President of the Security Council, took the initiative in convening the first-ever meeting of the Council at head of state/government level. This represented an unprecedented recommitment, at the highest political level, to the purposes and principles of the UN Charter.

The meeting invited the UN Secretary General to prepare a report on ways in which the organisation could reinforce its capacity for preventive diplomacy, peacekeeping and peacemaking. The Secretary General's report, under the title of *Agenda for Peace*, was published in June 1992 and welcomed by the Security Council.

Britain supported the report's call for:

—greater collaboration between the United Nations and regional organisations;

—states to accept without reservation before the year 2000 the general jurisdiction of the International Court of Justice; and

—greater co-ordination between UN specialised agencies in dealing with circumstances contributing to a dispute or conflict.

The report also suggested that UN member states should make forces available to the Security Council on a permanent basis.

UN Peacekeeping

Increasingly, parties to regional conflicts tend to look to the UN for solutions. Peacekeeping is one of the key tools at the UN's disposal for helping parties to such disputes resolve their differences.

At the beginning of 1992 there were about 12,000 troops deployed on UN peacekeeping missions: in the wake of new operations in Cambodia, Somalia, former Yugoslavia and Rwanda this figure increased to more than 700,000 by the summer of 1994.

In a report in March 1994, the UN Secretary General set out the steps taken to improve the UN's capacity to launch and manage peacekeeping operations, including the enhancement of its information and planning capabilities, and suggested certain definitions:

Preventive Diplomacy: action to prevent disputes from arising between parties, to prevent existing disputes from escalating into conflicts and to limit the spread of conflicts when they occur.

Peacemaking: diplomatic action to bring hostile parties to a negotiated agreement through peaceful means.

Peacekeeping: a UN presence in the field (normally including military and civilian personnel), with the consent of the parties to a dispute, to implement or monitor the arrangements relating to the control of conflicts (such as ceasefires and separation of forces) and their resolution, or to protect the delivery of humanitarian relief.

Peace Enforcement: action under Chapter VII of the UN Charter (see p. 67), including the use of armed force, to maintain or restore international peace and security in situations where the Security Council has determined the existence of a threat to peace, breach of the peace or act of aggression.

The UN is unable to intervene everywhere since it can launch a new peacekeeping mission only when personnel, money and equipment for a successful operation are available. Putting together a complex operation with its civilian and military elements usually takes several months. Another difficulty is that only a small number of member states, of which Britain is one, pay their assessed contributions to UN peacekeeping promptly and in full. Because of the UN's resulting financial problems, those states which provide troops have little prospect of reimbursement for their contributions.

When the UN is considering the launch of new peacekeeping missions, the Security Council must examine on a case-by-case basis whether:

—a clear political goal exists which can be reflected in the mandate;

—a precise mandate for the mission can be formulated;

—there is a ceasefire and a genuine peace process; and

—there is a threat to international peace and security.

The key to successful peacekeeping will remain the need to get the consent of the warring factions and to maintain the impartiality of the mission.

Britain and UN Peacekeeping

Britain is actively involved in efforts to strengthen UN peacekeeping operations.

In April 1994 Britain and France put forward proposals to the UN on ways of addressing potential conflicts before they become a reality. Both countries offered to provide personnel with experience relevant to regional problems, politics, languages, humanitarian relief, international law, communications and logistics. In addition the British and French Governments said that they would provide equipment for use in preventive diplomacy missions. The British-French proposal envisages that such missions would be established on the initiative of the UN Secretary General in order to defuse tensions by mediation and promote dialogue between the parties involved.

In September 1994 Britain had troops or observers deployed in Cyprus, former Yugoslavia, Georgia, on the Iraq-Kuwait border, and in Rwanda.

Cyprus

The UN Peacekeeping Force in Cyprus (UNFICYP) was established in 1964 to prevent the recurrence of fighting between the Greek and Turkish Cypriot communities. Since the serious hostilities in 1974, when Turkish forces occupied the northern part of the island, UNFICYP has been responsible for maintaining the ceasefire and control of the buffer zone between the two communities. It also carries out humanitarian functions.

Britain provides the largest contingent—about 420 personnel—to the UN force. The British garrison on Cyprus provides logistic support for all UN forces on the island and for other UN peacekeeping forces in the Middle East.

Former Yugoslavia

Croatia

In the early 1990s the federal state of Yugoslavia broke up into various independent states, some of which were ethnically divided. As a consequence political instability increased throughout the area and ethnic violence became widespread. Serb and Croatian forces, for instance, clashed in Croatia while in Bosnia and Herzegovina a three-cornered civil war developed between Serbs, Croats and Bosnian Government forces.

In September 1991 a special foreign ministers' meeting of the UN Security Council called on all states to implement immediately a 'general and complete embargo on all deliveries of weapons and military equipment to Yugoslavia'. Resolution 713, sponsored by Britain and four other Council members, appealed to all parties to settle disputes peacefully through negotiations at the Conference on Yugoslavia, organised by the European Community, now the European Union. A UN special envoy, Cyrus Vance, was appointed as the UN Secretary General's personal representative to promote peace in former Yugoslavia.

In December 1991 the Security Council endorsed the Secretary General's offer to send a small group, including military personnel, to Croatia in order to carry forward preparations for possible peacekeeping. The first UN monitors arrived in Zagreb on 18 December. Subsequently a UN group of military liaison officers arrived in January 1992 to try to maintain a ceasefire between Serbs and Croats.

Arrangements for this ceasefire were worked out by Mr Vance with Serbia and Croatia. As part of this agreement the UN Security Council adopted unanimously resolution 743 in February 1992. This led to the creation of a UN Protection Force (UNPROFOR) of some 13,000 troops and over 1,000 police and civilians in Croatia to monitor the ceasefire agreement. The UN force was asked to create three UN-protected areas in and around those regions of Croatia largely populated and controlled by Serbs. In these areas the UN force's functions were to:

—monitor the ceasefire and oversee demilitarisation and the withdrawal of forces;

—ensure that the local administration and the forces for the maintenance of public order accurately reflected the ethnic composi-
tion of the region; and

—ensure the maintenance of law and order and the status quo.

In October 1992 the UN force was requested to monitor
arrangements for the complete withdrawal of the Yugoslav federal
army from Croatia, the demilitarisation of southern Croatia near
Dubrovnik and the removal of heavy weapons from areas of Croatia
and Montenegro.

Medical personnel from the British armed forces joined the
UN peacekeeping force in Croatia following an announcement by
the Defence Secretary, Malcolm Rifkind, in April 1992. The 260-
strong unit, supported by other troops, was sent in four detach-
ments, with its headquarters based in Zagreb. The unit's main
tasks were to provide casualty evacuation by ambulance or heli-
copter and to supplement the medical support of the UN battalions. The unit was withdrawn in September 1993.

Bosnia and Herzegovina

In March 1992 a referendum in Bosnia and Herzegovina voted in
favour of an independent and autonomous republic. Some 37 per
cent of the electorate, mainly consisting of Serbs, did not take part
in the vote on the grounds that the republic could be dominated by
Muslims. Shortly after the referendum Serb forces, aided by the
Serb-dominated Yugoslav federal army, resorted to violence by
overrunning large parts of Bosnia, driving many Muslims from
their homes in waves of ethnic cleansing. Within weeks the Bosnian

capital, Sarajevo, was besieged by Serbian forces who repeatedly shelled the civilian population.

On 15 May 1992 the UN Security Council passed resolution 752 calling for an end to the fighting in Bosnia and the cessation of outside interference by Serbia and Croatia. Two weeks later the Council voted for resolution 757, proposed by Britain and four other states, which condemned the failure of Serbia to take effective action to fulfil resolution 752. The new resolution also called upon any elements of the Croatian army still present in Bosnia to withdraw. The Council requested all UN member states to impose immediate sanctions on Serbia including a trade embargo, a freeze on Serbian financial and economic assets and suspension of cultural and sporting relations.

These sanctions were enforced by a naval force deployed in the Adriatic by members of the North Atlantic Treaty Organisation (NATO) and the Western European Union (WEU), including Britain.

In recent months a contact group consisting of Britain, France, Germany, Russia and the United States has sought to build on earlier diplomatic efforts during 1992 and 1993 to promote a settlement. Under a plan worked out by the group, Bosnia and Herzegovina would be divided, 51 per cent going to the Muslim and Croat populations and the rest to the Bosnian Serbs. Although the plan was accepted by the Bosnian Government, it was turned down by the Bosnian Serbs.

UNPROFOR's role in Bosnia and Herzegovina is to provide support on the ground to underpin international efforts to broker a lasting peace between the warring parties. In June 1992 the Security Council requested UNPROFOR to ensure the security and functioning of Sarajevo airport. This and subsequent resolutions constituting UNPROFOR's mandate fall into five broad areas:

—security and functioning of Sarajevo airport and delivery of humanitarian aid to the city and the surrounding areas;

—monitoring ceasefires in Sarajevo and Bosnia brokered by the UN;

—protective support for UN efforts to deliver humanitarian relief throughout Bosnia and Herzegovina;

—protection of safe areas, as set out in a 1993 Security Council resolution; and

—monitoring the military situation and a no-fly zone over Bosnia and Herzegovina to prevent the use of aircraft in the conflict.

Although UNPROFOR has been authorised by the Security Council to use 'all necessary measures' to ensure the delivery of humanitarian relief and to protect the safe areas, it has maintained its impartiality in its efforts to achieve these goals.

UNPROFOR's total military and civilian strength is 34,500, of whom 18,000 are deployed in Bosnia and Herzegovina. The main contributors of troops to UNPROFOR are France (5,800), Britain (3,500), Jordan (3,500), The Netherlands (2,000) and Canada (2,000).

British Contribution

The British contribution consists of two armoured infantry battalion groups, supported by a logistics unit based on two Royal Fleet Auxiliary ships, and 19 military observers. This includes an engineer squadron and first-line logistic support and a mortar-locating radar unit. Four Royal Navy Sea King helicopters provide support to the battalions. RAF (Royal Air Force) Hercules transport aircraft makes regular aid flights into Sarajevo. The RAF contributes airborne early-warning aircraft and Tornado planes in order to monitor and enforce the no-fly zone. A squadron of eight

Jaguar aircraft, based in Italy, assists NATO in providing close air support to UNPROFOR in pursuit of its humanitarian mandate and in defence of its forces in the safe areas.

The Gulf Crisis

Iraq's invasion and military occupation of Kuwait in mid-1990 provoked not only condemnation but also unprecedented co-operation in the international community to reverse the aggression.[2] A UN-sponsored multinational military force was assembled under UN authorisation in the Gulf region during the months after August 1990. Britain's contribution to this force—some 45,000 personnel and their equipment—was the largest of any European country.

When it became clear that Iraq would respond neither to a series of Security Council resolutions nor to other diplomatic initiatives, armed force was initiated by the international coalition in mid-January 1991. Following a brief and successful campaign, the coalition forced Iraq to leave Kuwait and hostilities ceased at the end of February.

As part of the agreement ending military action, the Security Council authorised the creation of a Special Commission to supervise the elimination of Iraq's weapons of mass destruction and set out a number of other ceasefire conditions. UN economic sanctions against Iraq, introduced in August 1990, still apply because of the Iraqi Government's failure to comply fully with these conditions.

A demilitarised zone extending 10 km into Iraq and 5 km into Kuwait is monitored by a UN observer unit, UNIKOM, to which Britain contributes 15 military personnel. It was set up to deter violations of the boundary and to observe hostile or potentially hostile actions. A UN Boundary Commission has determined the international border between the two countries.

[2] For further information see *Britain and the Gulf Crisis* (Aspects of Britain: HMSO, 1993).

Britain has taken an active part since 1991 in helping, with the United States and France, to apply UN-approved no-fly zones over Iraq designed to monitor the actions of the Iraqi regime and deter military attacks against civilians in southern and northern areas of the country.

Rwanda

In August 1994 Britain began to deploy a 630-strong military logistic contingent to serve with the UN Assistance Mission in Rwanda (UNAMIR). UNAMIR was set up to monitor the implementation of the Arusha Agreement of June 1993 and was strengthened to help tackle the crisis brought about by the renewed outbreak of internal violence within the country in May 1994.

The British contingent, deployed for three months, comprised a field ambulance as well as elements of the Royal Engineers (RE) and the Royal Electrical and Mechanical Engineers (REME).

Arms Control

Since its inception the UN has had responsibilities in connection with arms control and disarmament, although it has not been involved directly in negotiations between the United States and the former Soviet Union (and more recently Russia) on nuclear arms and conventional forces. The question of arms control is, however, regularly discussed by the UN General Assembly and other relevant forums.

UN Forums

Britain contributes actively to the work of the Conference (formerly Committee) on Disarmament and its sub-groups and of the Disarmament Commission.

The Conference, which is the sole multilateral negotiating forum on disarmament issues, is an autonomous body with close links to the UN. It has 38 member countries representing all areas of the world, including the five nuclear weapon states (Britain, the People's Republic of China, France, the Russian Federation and the United States). It meets for about six months each year, working by consensus, and reports annually to the UN General Assembly. The Conference's Secretary General is appointed by the UN Secretary General.

The Disarmament Commission is a deliberative body of the whole UN membership established to make recommendations on arms control, and to follow up the decisions of the special sessions on disarmament. Unlike the Conference on Disarmament, it has no negotiating authority.

The First Committee of the General Assembly, composed of all UN member states, convenes each autumn in New York to consider arms control and disarmament matters. It holds general debates and adopts resolutions on specific aspects of arms-control issues on its agenda. Decisions are taken on the basis of majority votes although resolutions passed are not binding on member states.

During First Committee sessions the British Disarmament Delegation in Geneva transfers to New York. It liaises closely with NATO partners and often votes, and makes joint statements, with Britain's European Union partners.

General Assembly Special Sessions

Britain took part in three special sessions of the General Assembly devoted to disarmament in 1978, 1982 and 1988. At the first, Britain, with other western nations, maintained that the aim throughout the disarmament negotiations should be undiminished security at the lowest possible level of armaments and military forces, and this was endorsed in the session's final document. Neither the Second nor the Third Special Session was able to reach agreement on a plan of action. Nevertheless, Britain played a full and constructive role based on five principles:

—the relationship between disarmament and security;

—the need to address the underlying causes of military confrontation;

—verification;

—transparency; and

—realism.

UN Conference on Disarmament and Development, 1987

Britain took an active part in the UN Conference on Disarmament and Development which took place in New York in August and September 1987. The British approach was based on a commitment to both processes, each for its own sake, and a belief that there is no single automatic link between them. Britain also argued that any consideration of the relationship between disarmament and development must take into account a crucial third element, that of security.

The final document, adopted by consensus, reflected some of these concerns, containing a section on the philosophical relationship between disarmament and development, a section on the economic and social implications of military spending and an action programme. The 58 participating states reaffirmed their commitment to allocate a portion of resources released through disarmament for development, especially in poor countries.

Treaties

Britain is party to most of the agreements which have been concluded on multilateral arms control, including the Nuclear Non-Proliferation Treaty (NPT), the Biological and Toxin Weapons Convention and the Chemical Weapons Convention.

Nuclear Non-Proliferation

The NPT Treaty is the cornerstone of international efforts to prevent the spread of nuclear arms. It was open for signature in 1968 and entered into force in 1970. The Treaty recognised that there were five nuclear weapons states—Britain, China, France, the then

Soviet Union and the United States—and asked all other states to renounce nuclear weapons. In order for verification of renunciation to take place, these countries were also requested to accept safeguards applied by the International Atomic Energy Agency (IAEA). More than 160 states are party to the NPT, including the five nuclear weapons states, virtually all other industrialised countries and many developing countries. The IAEA has the right to conduct special investigations of suspected, but undeclared, nuclear sites. In addition the major nuclear exporters implement agreed controls on nuclear exports.

In 1995 a conference of states party to the NPT will decide by how long the Treaty should be extended. Britain's objective is to secure its indefinite extension.

The nuclear weapons states are continuing to take steps to control their own nuclear arsenals, through negotiated measures and unilateral actions. The latter include Britain's decisions to restrict the maximum number of warheads on its new Trident nuclear missiles and not to replace aircraft-dropped nuclear bombs when they come to the end of their service. Britain and the other nuclear weapons states are also negotiating to ban nuclear testing and are discussing ways of ending the production for nuclear-explosive purposes of highly enriched uranium and plutonium which are two key materials for making nuclear weapons.

Other treaties to which Britain is a party include:

—the 1959 Antarctic Treaty, which was the first treaty to put into practice the concept of a nuclear-weapon-free zone (later applied to the seabed, outer space and Latin America); and

—the 1963 Partial Test Ban Treaty, banning nuclear tests in the atmosphere, in outer space and under water (but not underground).

Biological Weapons

The use of biological weapons in war was banned by the 1925 Geneva Protocol, although countries were still allowed to develop, produce and possess them. Controls were strengthened by the 1972 Biological and Toxin Weapons Convention whose signatories completely renounced biological weapons. Britain and more than 130 other countries are signatories. The international community continues to press for universal adherence to the Convention and compliance with its provisions. The main problem is the lack of any effective verification provisions.

A review conference in 1991 introduced confidence-building measures providing for exchange of information between parties to the Convention, and also set up an expert group to identify and examine potential verification measures from a scientific and technical standpoint. The findings of this group were considered by a special conference of parties to the Convention in September 1994 with a view to reaching agreement on arrangements for verification.

Chemical Weapons

The 1925 Geneva Protocol also banned the use of chemical weapons because of the widespread revulsion at their use during the First World War. The Chemical Weapons Convention, introducing a ban on their development, production and possession, opened for signature in January 1993. More than 150 states have signed the Convention, including Britain. It will come into force six months after 65 countries have ratified it.

During the negotiations Britain pressed strongly for adequate verification measures and played a significant part in developing them. The final text of the Convention contains a thorough set of such measures, including declarations, routine inspections and challenge inspections. A Preparatory Commission is working to set up the future organisation for the prohibition of chemical weapons, which will be responsible for international implementation of the Convention.

Provision of Military Information

A major British initiative at the UN has been to encourage the provision of objective information on military matters. Reporting in 1984, a UN study on conventional disarmament— made up of non-governmental experts (including one from Britain)—emphasised the danger posed by modern conventional weapons. The study concluded that it was the responsibility of all states to participate in steps aimed at halting the current worldwide build-up.

The British Government welcomed many of the report's conclusions but pointed to the failure of some states to provide the study with any information and data on their military activities. Without openness and transparency on these, it said, there could be no increase in confidence and no successful disarmament negotiations.

To further this principle, Britain tabled a resolution at the First Committee of the 1986 UN General Assembly on the provision of objective information on military matters. It also co-sponsored a number of other successful resolutions, including one on guidelines for confidence-building measures, and another on verification of disarmament agreements.

Britain played an important part in establishing the UN's Register of Conventional Arms which is based on an idea put forward by the Prime Minister, John Major, in April 1991 after the expulsion of Iraqi forces from Kuwait. The Register covers seven categories of weapons judged to be of key importance for major offensive operations. The aim of the Register is to introduce more openness into the international arms trade and help to build confidence.

Human Rights

Britain has consistently supported UN efforts to promote human rights through the establishment of internationally accepted standards.[3] The UN Charter states that one purpose of the UN is to achieve international co-operation in promoting and encouraging respect for human rights and for fundamental freedoms for all.

Britain believes that expressions of concern about violations of human rights are matters of international responsibility and do not constitute interference in another state's internal affairs. UN members pledge themselves to take joint and separate action in co-operation with the UN to promote universal respect for, and observance of, human rights and fundamental freedoms, without distinction as to race, sex, language or religion.

Universal Declaration of Human Rights

Fundamental human rights provisions are set out in the Universal Declaration of Human Rights proclaimed by the General Assembly in 1948. The Universal Declaration, however, is not a legally binding document. In 1966, therefore, the General Assembly adopted two international covenants placing legal obligations on those states ratifying or acceding to them. The covenants came into force in 1976, Britain ratifying both in the same year.

[3] For further details see *Human Rights* (Aspects of Britain: HMSO, 1992).

International Covenant on Economic, Social and Cultural Rights

State parties to the International Covenant on Economic, Social and Cultural Rights are bound to promote the full realisation of these rights which include the right to:

—work;

—fair wages and an adequate standard of living;

—social security;

—education;

—the highest attainable health care standards;

—form and join trade unions; and

—participate in cultural life.

States who are party to the Covenant report to the UN Economic and Social Council on measures taken to promote these rights. ECOSOC's Committee on Economic, Social and Cultural Rights examines the reports in public session.

International Covenant on Civil and Political Rights

The International Covenant on Civil and Political Rights includes recognition of the right to:

—life;

—freedom from torture or cruel, inhuman or degrading treatment;

—freedom from slavery;

—security of person and freedom from arbitrary arrest and detention;

—freedom of movement;

—freedom from arbitrary expulsion;

—equality before the law;

—privacy;

—freedom of thought and religion;

—peaceful assembly;

—freedom of association, including trade union membership;

—take part in the conduct of public affairs;

—liberty; and

—freedom of expression.

Derogations from some of these obligations are permitted in time of an emergency threatening the life of a nation provided that these are justified by the situation. No derogation is permitted from certain articles such as those providing for the right to life, the prohibitions on torture and slavery and the right to freedom of thought, conscience or religion.

The Covenant provides for a UN Human Rights Committee—established in 1976—of 18 independent experts to examine publicly reports by the parties on progress made in implementing the Covenant's provisions. The Committee also considers claims on non-compliance with the Covenant by one state party against another and by individuals against their own country. Britain, in conformity with its obligations, submits regular reports to the Committee on the measures taken to give effect to these rights.

Other Conventions

Britain is also a party to a number of UN conventions designed to implement specific rights set out in the Universal Declaration.

Convention against Torture and Other Cruel, Inhuman or Degrading Treatment or Punishment

The Convention, which entered into force in 1987, obliges states parties to ensure the total abolition of torture and other cruel, inhuman treatment or punishment. A Committee against Torture monitors compliance and is composed of ten independent experts. The Committee has power to examine publicly reports submitted by states on the implementation of their intentions. With the agreement of the state concerned, it can make on-the-spot inquiries in cases where it receives information that torture is being practised systematically. The Committee can also consider claims of non-compliance by one state party against another, as well as complaints by individuals.

Racial Discrimination

The International Convention on the Elimination of All Forms of Racial Discrimination entered into force in 1969. Parties to the Convention are obliged to eliminate racial discrimination, promote understanding among all races and ensure that public authorities act accordingly. In addition they must guarantee the right of equality before the law and ensure protection and remedies against acts of racial discrimination which violate human rights.

An 18-member committee examines publicly reports made by states parties on their efforts to observe the Convention. It can also consider claims of violations by a state party made by individuals under the jurisdiction of that state or by another state party.

Discrimination Against Women

The Convention on the Elimination of All Forms of Discrimination against Women, which entered into force in 1981, obliges state parties to seek to eliminate discrimination against women in all fields. Positive discrimination such as temporary measures designed to accelerate equality between men and women is allowed.

A 23-member committee publicly examines reports submitted by states on fulfilment of their obligations, although there is no procedure for examination by the committee of state-to-state or individual complaints.

Others
Other UN human rights conventions to which Britain is a party include those regarding:

—prevention of genocide;

—the abolition of slavery and forced labour;

—the status of refugees and stateless persons;

—the political rights of women;

—consent to marriage;

—the right to organise and collective bargaining; and

—freedom of association.

Britain is currently a member of the UN Commission on Human Rights which considers complaints of violations of human rights. Investigations can be proposed by any member government and are decided upon by vote of the entire Commission.

British independent experts also sit on other UN committees concerned with the observance of human rights.

World Conference on Human Rights

Britain attended the UN Conference on Human Rights which was held in Vienna in June 1993. The purpose of the Conference was for the international community to make a fresh and clear commitment to the implementation of human rights.

The Environment

UN Conference on the Environment and Development

The 1992 UN Conference on the Environment and Development, or 'Earth Summit', was held in Rio de Janeiro (Brazil) in June 1992. Heads of government from over 100 nations addressed the complex relationship between environmental degradation and development. They drew up a comprehensive action programme for international activity into the next century (Agenda 21).

Among the major achievements of the Conference were:

— the signing of effective conventions on climate change and biological diversity;

— agreement on principles for sustaining management of all types of forests;

— approval of a declaration on environmental rights and obligations; and

— agreement on methods of channelling more financial assistance to help developing countries to meet environmental challenges.

At the Conference Britain launched three initiatives:

— the Darwin Initiative for the Survival of Species, which provides funding for British organisations such as the Royal Botanic Gardens at Kew and Edinburgh, the Natural History Museum in London and the World Conservation Monitoring Centre at Cambridge to assist conservation overseas and help countries meet their obligations under the Biodiversity Convention. Some £9 million was made available over the first four years of the Initiative, and 53 projects have been funded including training, conservation and scientific study;

—the Technology Partnership Initiative, which allows developing countries better access to environmentally sound technologies, by sharing information and by direct contacts with British companies; and

—the convening of an international conference for non-governmental organisations, which was held in Manchester in September 1993 and was attended by over 300 participants from more than 85 countries.

The UN Commission on Sustainable Development was set up in 1993 to monitor progress on implementing Earth Summit commitments. Britain is an elected member of the Commission until 1996. One of Britain's main contributions to the Commission's work programme is a joint initiative with India which will establish a bridge between the developed and developing world on forestry issues.

New Environmental Forums

Britain is closely involved in the work of the UN Intergovernmental Negotiating Committee for the Framework Convention on Climate Change. The Committee is working to implement the agreements made at the Earth Summit. Britain is also working to achieve agreement on the conservation of biological diversity.

Britain contributed over £40.3 million to the pilot phase of a new fund—the Global Environment Facility—set up by the World

Bank, the UN Environment Programme (UNEP) and the UNDP to help developing countries play their part in protecting the global environment. In March 1994 Britain agreed to contribute a further £89.5 million to the fund, making it the fifth largest contributor. This reflects the Government's belief that the fund has a major role to play in improving the international response to global and environmental threats.

UN Environment Programme

UNEP has supported a number of international conventions and agreements. In 1985 the Vienna Convention on the Protection of the Ozone Layer was adopted, followed two years later by the signing of the Montreal Protocol. This aims to cut by half the use of certain chlorofluorocarbons (CFCs) damaging to the atmosphere by the end of the century. At meetings in London in 1990 and Copenhagen in 1992, the Protocol's signatories agreed to the faster phase-out of CFCs and the introduction of controls on ozone-depleting substances not previously covered. A multilateral fund has been established to help developing country parties meet their obligations under the Protocol. The British contribution to this fund is up to a maximum of $40 million.

The Basel Convention, negotiated by UNEP in 1989, provides controls on the international movement and disposal of hazardous wastes, and reflects the British Government's policy that developed countries should become self-sufficient in the final disposal of such waste. Britain has been making voluntary financial contributions of $50,000 on an annual basis since 1990 and is making mandatory contributions from May 1994.

Narcotics Control and Measures Against Illicit Drug Trafficking

UN Action

The UN has for some time played a leading role in international legislation and activity against drugs.

1961 and 1971 Conventions

Two UN Conventions, which Britain has ratified, regulate legal trading in drugs, so as to ensure that only sufficient drugs to meet legitimate needs are available.

The 1961 UN Single Convention on Narcotic Drugs, amended by its 1972 Protocol, provides for controls over opium and its derivatives, such as heroin and morphine, and other drugs likely to cause similar ill-effects, such as methadone, cocaine and cannabis. The 1971 UN Convention on Psychotropic Substances provides for similar controls over a wide range of synthetic drugs which act on the central nervous system (hallucinogens, stimulants, sedatives and tranquillisers).

Parties to the Conventions are required to apply stringent controls over drug production, manufacture, distribution and availability, both for domestic consumption and for export. They also undertake to co-operate closely with the UN in ensuring the effective operation of the Conventions; for example, by operating a comprehensive licensing system for legal transactions and by providing regular statistical returns.

1988 Convention

The UN Convention Against Illicit Traffic in Narcotic Drugs and Psychotropic Substances was signed in Vienna in 1988 by 43 countries, including Britain which played a leading role during the four years preparation of the Convention. Britain ratified it in June 1991.

The Convention requires signatories to introduce legislation making all aspects of illicit trafficking in drugs, including the laundering of profits from these activities, criminal offences. It contains provisions on:

—tracing, freezing and confiscating traffickers' assets;

—the extradition of suspected traffickers;

—mutual legal assistance in criminal proceedings relating to trafficking offences;

—permitting detected consignments of illicit drugs to proceed to their destination in order to identify and arrest the principals behind the traffic;

—preventing the diversion from the legal market of essential chemicals used in illicit drug production; and

—stopping and searching ships suspected of being used for drug trafficking in international waters.

In accordance with the Convention's provisions, Britain has introduced new powers to:

—co-operate with other countries in the investigation and prosecution of criminal offences;

—strengthen British provisions against money laundering and for confiscation of the proceeds of drug trafficking;

—stop and search ships suspected of being used for drug trafficking in international waters; and

—make drug trafficking offences fully extraditable.

UN Drugs Control Structure

Britain has long played a part in the various UN bodies concerned with the problem of drugs misuse. The main ones are the:

UN Commission on Narcotic Drugs

This body, which is the principal drug policy-making body of the UN, was established in 1946. It advises ECOSOC and prepares international agreements on drugs matters. Its responsibilities include varying the list of drugs under international control, advising other UN bodies on strategies and priorities, and examining proposals for specific UN projects in the drugs field.

Britain has been a member of the Commission since its inception, providing experts for meetings and working groups, and contributing to proposals for conventions.

International Narcotics Control Board

The Board's establishment was provided for in the 1961 UN Single Convention on Narcotic Drugs which came into force in 1964. Its task is to monitor the legal international and domestic movement of narcotic drugs and psychotropic substances for medical and scientific needs, and to promote compliance by governments with the various drug control treaties. The 13 members of the Board serve in their personal capacity, not as representatives of their governments. British experts have frequently served on the Board.

UN International Drug Control Programme

In 1991 the UN Secretary General set up a new single body, the UN International Drug Control Programme (UNDCP), to take over and further develop the functions formerly carried out by the Division of Narcotic Drugs, the secretariat of the International Narcotics Control Board and the UN Fund for Drug Abuse Control (UNFDAC).

UNDCP was given the leading role in co-ordinating UN action against drug misuse. It also took on the responsibility for monitoring implementation of the three UN Conventions on drugs and for carrying out technical assistance programmes, mainly to developing countries, in areas such as income substitution, law enforcement and drug-demand reduction.

Some 90 per cent of UNDCP's funding is derived from voluntary contributions, and Britain is a major donor. The British Government believes that the creation of UNDCP will enhance international efforts to combat the drug problem and reduce duplication.

General Assembly High-level Plenary Meetings on Drugs

Britain took an active part in the High-level Plenary Meetings on Drugs at the UN General Assembly in 1993 at which two important resolutions were adopted. The first sought additional measures to strengthen international co-operation against illicit drug activities and the second called for full implementation of the UN

Global Plan of Action (GPA) and the UN system-wide Action Plan on drug-abuse control (SWAP). The GPA encourages UN member states who have not already done so to ratify the 1988 Convention (see p. 49), and the SWAP calls for all UN bodies to introduce drug-related programmes in their activities.

Efforts to Stem Drug Production and Trafficking

Apart from direct assistance to individual governments, much of Britain's contribution to the international fight against drugs is channelled through UNDCP. In common with that of most other developed nations, British aid is designed to help the many countries which do not have the necessary resources, experience or expertise.

An important form of assistance is for rural development, crop substitution and eradication—all aimed at preventing illicit drugs from being produced in the first place. The aim is to strengthen the rural economies of producer countries, so that the inhabitants should not have to grow opium or coca to secure an acceptable standard of living. Recipients of UNDCP aid for rural development projects include Pakistan, Bolivia and Laos.

Working for Children

UN Convention on the Rights of the Child

The Convention on the Rights of the Child was unanimously adopted by the UN General Assembly in 1989, and ratified by Britain in 1991. It contains a comprehensive set of international legal norms for the protection and well-being of children.

The Convention says that:

—all the rights in the Convention apply to all children equally whatever their race, sex, religion, language, disability, opinion or family background;

—when adults or organisations make decisions which affect children they must always think first about what would be best for the child; and

—children have the right to say what they think about anything which affects them and they must be listened to. For example, when courts or other official bodies are making decisions which affect children they must listen to what the children want and feel.

Regarding civil and political rights, the Convention says that children have the right to:

—a name and a nationality at birth;

—freedom of expression;

—freedom of thought, conscience and religion;

—personal privacy;

—access to information;

—protection from violence and harmful treatment; and

—fair treatment before the law.

A child's economic, social, cultural and protective rights include the right to:

—life;

—an adequate standard of living;

—day-to-day care;

—health and healthcare;

—a healthy environment;

—education and leisure; and

—protection from exploitation.

Britain's Commitment

The British Government is committed to support the Convention, the philosophy of which is very closely reflected in the Children Act 1989. Two of the main rights in the Convention—that the best interests of the child should be the primary consideration and that the voice of the child should be heard—are embodied as central tenets of the Act. By itself, the Act meets in whole or in part the obligations contained in 13 of the 40 main articles of the Convention.

In 1994 and every five years after that, the Government will send the UN Committee on the Rights of the Child a report explaining how it is putting the Convention into practice. It also recognises the importance of working together with poorer countries to make life better for children living there.

The Government has entered certain reservations, meaning that it will not necessarily follow the Convention in every respect. One reservation is that the Government regards the Convention as applying only after a live birth. Others are about immigration and nationality, employment law affecting 16 to 18-year-olds and the separation of children from adults in prison.

UN World Summit for Children

Hosted by UNICEF (see p. 20), the World Summit for Children took place in New York in September 1990. A declaration on the survival, protection and development of children was approved by 72 countries, including Britain. At the Summit, the heads of state or government agreed to set specific goals for the 1990s and to implement a ten-point plan of action to achieve them.

The first goal was to urge all governments to promote ratification of the UN Convention on the Rights of the Child. Other goals, to be achieved by the year 2000, included:

—reducing the deaths of children under five throughout the world by a third;

—halving the number of maternal deaths;

—reducing malnutrition among children under five by a half;

—providing universal access to safe drinking water and sanitation;

—providing universal access to basic education and completion of primary education by at least 80 per cent of primary-school age children; and

—protecting children in especially difficult circumstances. These include homeless children; victims of abuse, drugs, and armed conflict; refugee children; and children who are exploited sexually or as labourers.

Signatories of the declaration have committed themselves to making resources available to reach the stated goals. It was agreed that the UN agencies should monitor implementation of the plan, and that the UN Secretary General should carry out a review of progress in 1995.

Development Aid

The UN is one of the main vehicles for British international aid to developing countries.

The aid programme has seven main objectives, namely to:

—promote economic reform;

—increase productive capacity;

—promote good government;

—cut poverty;

—improve education and health;

—promote the status of women; and

—help developing countries tackle national environmental problems.

In 1992–93 about £145 million of British aid was channelled through UN development and humanitarian agencies, including £64 million in response to needs for humanitarian assistance. Britain has also intensified efforts to improve the effectiveness and efficiency of these agencies. Reform processes are under way in the UNDP, UNICEF and other major UN bodies.

The table below shows the total British contributions to the various UN aid agencies in 1992–93:

UN Disaster Relief	£37,577,000
UN Development Programme	£30,243,000
World Food Programme (Food Aid)	£14,621,000
World Health Organisation	£12,065,000
UN Children's Fund	£10,290,000
UN Population Fund	£9,423,000

UN Agency for Palestinian Refugees	£6,250,000
UN High Commissioner for Refugees	£5,500,000
Food and Agriculture Organisation	£5,457,000
UN Industrial Development Organisation	£5,336,000
UN Department of Humanitarian Affairs	£4,000,000
International Fund for Agricultural Development	£1,680,000
International Atomic Energy Authority	£563,000
World Food Programme (cash contributions)	£500,000
UN Industrial Development Fund	£346,000
UN Border Relief Operation (Thailand/Cambodia)	£200,000
UN Drug Control	£127,000
Other	£500,000

Appendix: Edited Extracts from the Charter of the United Nations

Chapter IV: The General Assembly

Composition

Article 9

1. The General Assembly shall consist of all the Members of the United Nations.

2. Each Member shall have not more than five representatives in the General Assembly.

Functions and Powers

Article 10

The General Assembly may discuss any questions or any matters within the scope of the present Charter or relating to the powers and functions of any organs provided for in the present Charter, and, except as provided in Article 12, may make recommendations to the Members of the United Nations or to the Security Council or to both on any such questions or matters.

Article 11

1. The General Assembly may consider the general principles of co-operation in the maintenance of international peace and security, including the principles governing disarmament and the regulation of armaments, and may make recommendations with regard to such principles to the Members or to the Security Council or to both.

2. The General Assembly may discuss any questions relating to the maintenance of international peace and security brought before it by any Member of the United Nations, or by the Security Council, or by a state which is not a Member of the United Nations in accordance with Article 35, paragraph 2, and, except as provided in Article 12, may make recommendations with regard to any such questions to the state or states concerned or to the Security Council or to both. Any such question on which action is necessary shall be referred to the Security Council by the General Assembly either before or after discussion.

3. The General Assembly may call the attention of the Security Council to situations which are likely to endanger international peace and security.

4. The powers of the General Assembly set forth in this Article shall not limit the general scope of Article 10.

Article 12
1. While the Security Council is exercising in respect of any dispute or situation the functions assigned to it in the present Charter, the General Assembly shall not make any recommendation with regard to that dispute or situation unless the Security Council so requests.

2. The Secretary General, with the consent of the Security Council, shall notify the General Assembly at each session of any matters relative to the maintenance of international peace and security which are being dealt with by the Security Council and shall similarly notify the General Assembly, or the Members of the United Nations if the General Assembly is not in session, immediately the Security Council ceases to deal with such matters.

Article 13
1. The General Assembly shall initiate studies and make recommendations for the purpose of:

a. promoting international co-operation in the political field and encouraging the progressive development of international law and its codification;

b. promoting international co-operation in the economic, social, cultural, educational, and health fields, and assisting in the realization of human rights and fundamental freedoms for all without distinction as to race, sex, language, or religion ...

Article 14

Subject to the provisions of Article 12, the General Assembly may recommend measures for the peaceful adjustment of any situation, regardless of origin, which it deems likely to impair the general welfare or friendly relations among nations, including situations resulting from a violation of the provisions of the present Charter setting forth the Purposes and Principles of the United Nations.

Article 15

1.   The General Assembly shall receive and consider annual and special reports from the Security Council; these reports shall include an account of the measures that the Security Council has decided upon or taken to maintain international peace and security.

2.   The General Assembly shall receive and consider reports from the other organs of the United Nations.

Article 16

The General Assembly shall perform such functions with respect to the international trusteeship system as are assigned to it ... including the approval of the trusteeship agreements for areas not designed as strategic.

Article 17

1.   The General Assembly shall consider and approve the budget of the Organisation.

2.   The expenses of the Organisation shall be borne by the Members as apportioned by the General Assembly.

3.   The General Assembly shall consider and approve any financial and budgetary arrangements with specialised agencies ... and shall examine the administrative budgets of such specialised agencies with a view to making recommendations to the agencies concerned.

Voting

Article 18

1.   Each member of the General Assembly shall have one vote.

2.   Decisions of the General Assembly on important questions shall be made by a two-thirds majority of the members present and voting. These questions shall include: recommendations with respect to the maintenance of international peace and security, the election of the non-permanent members of the Security Council, the election of the members of the Economic and Social Council, the election of members of the Trusteeship Council..., the admission of new Members to the United Nations, the suspension of the rights and privileges of membership, the expulsion of Members, questions relating to the operation of the trustee-ship system, and budgetary questions.

3.   Decisions on other questions, including the determination of additional categories of questions to be decided by a two-thirds majority, shall be made by a majority of the members present and voting.

Article 19

A member of the United Nations which is in arrears in the payment of its financial contributions to the Organisation shall have no vote in the General Assembly if the amount of its arrears equals or exceeds the amount of the contributions due from it for the preceding two full years. The General Assembly may, nevertheless, permit such a Member to vote if it is satisfied that the failure to pay is due to conditions beyond the control of the Member.

Procedure

Article 20

The General Assembly shall meet in regular annual sessions and in such special sessions as occasion may require. Special sessions shall be convoked by the Secretary General at the request of the Security Council or of a majority of the Members of the United Nations.

Article 21

The General Assembly shall adopt its own rules of procedure. It shall elect its President for each session.

Article 22

The General Assembly may establish such subsidiary organs as it deems necessary for the performance of its functions.

Chapter V: The Security Council

Composition

Article 23

1.   The Security Council shall consist of fifteen Members of the United Nations. The [People's] Republic of China, France, and Union of Soviet Socialist Republics,[a] the United Kingdom of Great Britain and Northern Ireland, and the United States of America shall be permanent members of the Security Council. The General Assembly shall elect ten other Members of the United Nations to be non-permanent members of the Security Council, due regard being specially paid, in the first instance to the contribution of Members of the United Nations to the maintenance of international peace and security and to the other purposes of the Organisation, and also to equitable geographical distribution.

2.   The non-permanent members of the Security Council shall be elected for a term of two years. In the first election of the non-permanent members after the increase of the membership of the Security Council from eleven to fifteen, two of the four additional members shall be chosen for a term of one year. A retiring member shall not be eligible for immediate re-election.

3.   Each member of the Security Council shall have one representative.

[a] Russia has assumed the international obligations of the former Soviet Union.

Functions and Powers

Article 24

1. In order to ensure prompt and effective action by the United Nations, its Members confer on the Security Council primary responsibility for the maintenance of international peace and security, and agree that in carrying out its duties under this responsibility the Security Council acts on their behalf.

2. In discharging these duties the Security Council shall act in accordance with the Purposes and Principles of the United Nations ...

3. The Security Council shall submit annual and, when necessary, special reports to the General Assembly for its consideration.

Article 25

The Members of the United Nations agree to accept and carry out the decisions of the Security Council in accordance with the present Charter.

Article 26

In order to promote the establishment and maintenance of international peace and security with the least diversion for armaments of the world's human and economic resources, the Security Council shall be responsible for formulating, with the assistance of the Military Staff Committee referred to in Article 47, plans to the submitted to the Members of the United Nations for the establishment of a system for the regulation of armaments.

Voting

Article 27

1. Each member of the Security Council shall have one vote.

2. Decisions of the Security Council on procedural matters shall be made by an affirmative vote of nine members.

3. Decisions of the Security Council on all other matters shall be made by an affirmative vote of nine members including the concurring votes of

the permanent members; provided that in decisions under Chapter VI, and under paragraph 3 of Article 52, a party to a dispute shall abstain from voting.

Procedure

Article 28

1.   The Security Council shall be so organised as to be able to function continuously. Each member of the Security Council shall for this purpose be represented at all times at the seat of the Organisation.

2.   The Security Council shall hold periodic meetings at which each of its members may, if it so desires, be represented by a member of the government or by some other specially designated representative.

3.   The Security Council may hold meetings at such places other than the seat of the Organisation as in its judgement will best facilitate its work.

Article 29

The Security Council may establish such subsidiary organs as it deems necessary for the performance of its functions.

Article 30

The Security Council shall adopt its own rules of procedure, including the method of selecting its President.

Article 31

Any Member of the United Nations which is not a member of the Security Council may participate, without vote, in the discussion of any question brought before the Security Council whenever the latter considers that the interests of that Member are specially affected.

Article 32

Any Member of the United Nations which is not a member of the Security Council or any state which is not a Member of the United Nations, if it is a party to a dispute under consideration by the Security Council, shall be invited to participate, without vote, in the discussion relating to the dispute. The Security Council shall lay down such conditions as it deems just for the participation of a state which is not a Member of the United Nations.

Chapter VI: Pacific Settlement of Disputes

Article 33

1. The parties to any dispute, the continuance of which is likely to endanger the maintenance of international peace and security, shall, first of all, seek a solution by negotiation, enquiry, mediation, conciliation, arbitration, judicial settlement, resort to regional agencies or arrangements, or other peaceful means of their own choice.

2. The Security Council shall, when it deems necessary, call upon the parties to settle their dispute by such means.

Article 34

The Security Council may investigate any dispute, or any situation which might lead to international friction or give rise to a dispute, in order to determine whether the continuance of the dispute or situation is likely to endanger the maintenance of international peace and security.

Article 35

1. Any Member of the United Nations may bring any dispute, or any situation of the nature referred to in Article 34, to the attention of the Security Council or of the General Assembly.

2. A state which is not a Member of the United Nations may bring to the attention of the Security Council or of the General Assembly any dispute to which it is a party if it accepts in advance, for the purposes of the dispute, the obligations of pacific settlement provided in the present Charter . . .

Article 36

1.   The Security Council may, at any stage of a dispute of the nature referred to in Article 33 or of a situation of like nature, recommend appropriate procedures or methods of adjustment.

2.   The Security Council should take into consideration any procedures for the settlement of the dispute which have already been adopted by the parties.

3.   In making recommendations under this Article the Security Council should also take into consideration that legal disputes should as a general rule be referred by the parties to the International Court of Justice in accordance with the provisions of the Statute of the Court.

Article 37

1.   Should the parties to a dispute of the nature referred to in Article 33 fail to settle it by the means indicated in that Article, they shall refer it to the Security Council.

2.   If the Security Council deems that the continuance of the dispute is in fact likely to endanger the maintenance of international peace and security, it shall decide whether to take action under Article 36 or to recommend such terms of settlement as it may consider appropriate.

Article 38

Without prejudice to the provisions of Articles 33 to 37, the Security Council may, if all the parties to any dispute so request, make recommendations to the parties with a view to a pacific settlement of the dispute.

Chapter VII: Action with Respect to Threats to the Peace, Breaches of the Peace, and Acts of Aggression

Article 39

The Security Council shall determine the existence of any threat to the peace, breach of the peace, or act of aggression and shall make recommendations, or decide what measures shall be taken in accordance with Articles 41 and 42, to maintain or restore international peace and security.

Article 40

In order to prevent an aggravation of the situation, the Security Council may, before making the recommendations or deciding upon the measures provided for in Article 39, call upon the parties concerned to comply with such provisional measures as it deems necessary or desirable. Such provisional measures shall be without prejudice to the rights, claims or position of the parties concerned. The Security Council shall duly take account of failure to comply with such provisional measures.

Article 41

The Security Council may decide what measures not involving the use of armed force are to be employed to give effect to its decisions, and it may call upon the Members of the United Nations to apply such measures. These may include complete or partial interruption of economic relations and of rail, sea, air, postal, telegraphic, radio and other means of communications, and the severance of diplomatic relations.

Article 42

Should the Security Council consider that measures provided for in Article 41 would be inadequate or have proved to be inadequate, it may take such action by air, sea or land forces as may be necessary to maintain or restore international peace and security. Such action may include demonstrations, blockade, and other operations by air, sea, or land forces of Members of the United Nations.

Article 43

1. All Members of the United Nations, in order to contribute to the maintenance of international peace and security, undertake to make available to the Security Council, on its call and in accordance with a special agreement or agreements, armed forces, assistance and facilities, including rights of passage, necessary for the purpose of maintaining international peace and security.

2.   Such agreement or agreements shall govern the numbers and types of forces, their degree of readiness and general location, and the nature of the facilities and assistance to be provided.

3.   The agreement or agreements shall be negotiated as soon as possible on the initiative of the Security Council. They shall be concluded between and Security Council and Members or between the Security Council and groups of Members and shall be subject to ratification by the signatory states in accordance with their respective constitutional processes.

Article 44

When the Security Council has decided to use force it shall, before calling upon a Member not represented on it to provide armed forces in fulfilment of the obligations assumed under Article 43, invite that Member, if the Member so desires, to participate in the decisions of the Security Council concerning the employment of contingents of that Member's armed forces.

Article 45

In order to enable the United Nations to take urgent military measures, Members shall hold immediately available national air force contingents for combined international enforcement action. The strength and degree of readiness of these contingents and plans for their combined action shall be determined, within the limits laid down in the special agreement or agreements referred to in Article 43, by the Security Council with the assistance of the Military Staff Committee.

Article 46

Plans for the application of armed force shall be made by the Security Council with the assistance of the Military Staff Committee.

Article 47

1.   There shall be established a Military Staff Committee to advise and assist the Security Council on all questions relating to the Security Council's military requirements for the maintenance of international

peace and security, the employment and command of forces placed at its disposal, the regulation of armaments, and possible disarmament.

2.   The Military Staff Committee shall consist of the Chiefs of Staff of the permanent members of the Security Council or their representatives. Any Member of the United Nations not permanently represented on the Committee shall be invited by the Committee to be associated with it when the efficient discharge of the Committee's responsibilities requires the participation of that Member in its work.

3.   The Military Staff Committee shall be responsible under the Security Council for the strategic direction of any armed forces placed at the disposal of the Security Council. Questions relating to the command of such forces shall be worked out subsequently.

4.   The Military Staff Committee, with the authorisation of the Security Council and after consultation with appropriate regional agencies, may establish regional sub-committees.

Article 48

1.   The action required to carry out the decisions of the Security Council for the maintenance of international peace and security shall be taken by all the Members of the United Nations or by some of them, as the Security Council may determine.

2.   Such decisions shall be carried out by the Members of the United Nations directly and through their action in the appropriate international agencies of which they are members.

Article 49

The Members of the United Nations shall join in affording mutual assistance in carrying out the measures decided upon by the Security Council.

Article 50

If preventive or enforcement measures against any state are taken by the Security Council, any other state, whether a Member of the United

Nations or not, which finds itself confronted with special economic problems arising from the carrying out of those measures shall have the right to consult the Security Council with regard to a solution of those problems.

Article 51
Nothing in the present Charter shall impair the inherent right of individual or collective self-defence if an armed attach occurs against a Member of the United Nations, until the Security Council has taken measures necessary to maintain international peace and security. Measures taken by Members in the exercise of this right of self-defence shall be immediately reported to the Security Council and shall not in any way affect the authority and responsibility of the Security Council under the present Charter to take at any time such action as it deems necessary in order to maintain or restore international peace and security.

Chapter VIII: Regional Arrangements

Article 52
1.   Nothing in the present Charter precludes the existence of regional arrangements or agencies for dealing with such matters relating to the maintenance of international peace and security as are appropriate for regional action, provided that such arrangements or agencies and their activities are consistent with the Purposes and Principles of the United Nations.

2.   The Members of the United Nations entering into such arrangements or constituting such agencies shall make every effort to achieve pacific settlement of local disputes through such regional arrangements or by such regional agencies before referring them to the Security Council.

3.   The Security Council shall encourage the development of pacific settlement of local disputes through such regional arrangements or by such regional agencies either on the initiative of the states concerned or by reference from the Security Council.

4.   This Article in no way impairs the application of Articles 34 and 35.

Further Reading

			£
Britain and the Gulf Crisis. Aspects of Britain. ISBN 0 11 701734 5.	HMSO	1993	£5
Human Rights. Aspects of Britain. ISBN 0 11 701665 9.	HMSO	1992	£6
The United Kingdom and the United Nations. Edited by Erik Jensen and Thomas Fisher.	Macmillan	1990	

Index

Printed in the UK for HMSO.
Dd.0298438, 11/94, C30, 56-6734, 5673.